STEP-BY-STEP

SPIRITUALITY FOR DEACONS

Deacon Eddie Ensley, Ph.D.

Abbey Press Publications

The stories from this book that involve people other than the author make use of composites created by the author from his experience with real people in his ministry. Names and details of the stories have been changed, and any similarity between names and stories of individuals in this book to individuals known to readers is purely coincidental.

Cover and book design by Mary E. Bolin.

ISBN 978-0-87029-562-1
Library of Congress 2014934996

Published by Abbey Press
1 Hill Drive St. Meinrad, IN 47577
Printed by Abbey Press in United States of America.
www.abbeypresspublications.com

This book is dedicated to Deacon George Foster,
director of the Diaconate Diocese of Savannah,
and his wife, Georgia Foster,
two people whose lives and love
have touched me deeply.

Contents

Foreword

I have known Deacon Eddie Ensley and his associate, Deacon Robert Herrmann, in a very special way. I was a pastor in the Archdiocese of Atlanta for many years and during that time I would invite priests, theologians, and others to conduct retreats or missions for the people. Upon learning of Deacon Ensley and reading a few of his books, I invited him and Robert to conduct retreats and missions over the course of a few years. The members of my parish and I were blessed by their presence, their message of love, acceptance of others, forgiveness, and their hope and joy in our faith.

As I read this new book on the spirituality of permanent deacons, it brought back to my memory the message delivered to my parish family. I witnessed the transformation of many as a result of their presence. The people discovered the richness of their own spiritual tradition, and that of the Church. In opening new insights into diaconal spirituality, Deacon Ensley writes, "Spirituality involves more than our religious side, more than our soul. It involves the whole of us, our work, our ministry, and our family." I believe each reader will experience a deeper and more meaningful prayer life.

This wonderful piece of work will give the reader a new understanding of prayer, of *lectio divina*, and the beauty of Sacred Scripture in one's prayer life. It will enable them to be engulfed in a deeper relationship with our Lord Jesus, allowing their lives to take on a new dimension, a new understanding of the phrase "becoming one with God" in prayer and in the journey of daily life.

Most Reverend Gregory John Hartmayer, O.F.M., Conv.
Bishop of the Diocese of Savannah

Chapter I

Letting God Saturate Our Lives With His Love

John, a deacon of around 60 who had come to the deacon retreat I helped lead, looked tense. His facial muscles were tight and his back slightly bent with anxiety. I later found out why: his wife Joyce had died 10 months before and recently his only child, a son, had moved his family across the continent because of a new job.

It was the end of a retreat Deacon Robert Herrmann and I helped lead for deacons and wives in the West. We spent the weekend talking about down-to-earth ways of praying, and I had just finished leading a contemplative-style meditation. We were drawn into a deep quiet, in which we felt God's love stir us and knit us back together. The presence of God filled our hearts so much that gentle tears streamed down both John's face and the faces of others.

During the retreat, John, along with others, had the chance to pray often, to journal, to make connections with old friends, to reflect on relationships and, most of all, embrace, in a deeper way, their call to *diakonia*—to servant-hood. John had especially needed this time with God and with others.

John told me early in the retreat that he had been on the brink of despair after his wife's death. The two of them had prayed together, entered the silence together, and said the *Liturgy of the Hours* together—and now she was gone and he was all alone. John said the retreat helped him to experience God's love without his wife being physically present, enabling him to let go of emotions he had long held tightly within.

John shared that during the meditation the first morning of the retreat, during which we imagined meeting Jesus. Jesus had taken John's hand and tension began to flow out of his body and soul. He bared his heart to old friends, especially those who had accompanied him through formation. They suggested that the several deacons in his hometown get together for Morning Prayer, spiritual sharing, and mutual support once a week. The other deacons had rushed in to reconnect with him and let him know how sorry they were for his losses and how much they wanted to renew friendships and be available for him as companions along the way.

John is an example of hundreds of lives I have seen transformed when people discover the practical, usable riches of our spiritual tradition.

The first point to make about spirituality for deacons, or for anyone for that matter, is that spirituality is not so much about climbing a ladder toward perfection or running an obstacle course successfully, as it is about grace—the love of God reaching down to us and elevating us. It is not about being a spiritual athlete, but about holding out a cup for God to fill it. It is so easy to fall into a Pelagian view of prayer and spirituality which would make us think that anything we gain from prayer or reflection is the result of our own hard work.

Spirituality and prayer are about letting God do what he wants to do most, which is to simply love us. God is an enormous and tremendous lover. His love is the ground of the cosmos, all creation, and our very selves. He loves us body and soul, down to the very cells of our fingernails. He wants us to say "yes" to that love, through his grace, love him in return, and love all that he loves.

God's enormous love became touchable, real, down-to-earth, everyday love in Jesus; it remains physical and tangible in the Eucharist.

Spirituality involves more than our religious side, more than our soul. It involves the whole of us, our work, our ministry, our family. There is not some special section in our hearts marked as "spiritual." True spirituality concerns our hurts, our gifts, our sexuality, and our relationships with others, especially the marginalized and the outcast.

In prayer, deacons take the whole context of their ministries and lives and let God soak it with the wonder of his caring.

All Christians, through baptism, share in both the priestly and servant ministry of Christ. Deacons, especially, are an icon or sign of Jesus' ministry as servant. At his last meal with his disciples, Jesus modeled the ministry of servant by washing the feet of his followers. He called them to be servants when he said to them that they should wash the feet of one another.

In down-to-earth, incarnational spirituality, we allow Jesus to wash our feet, and in turn wash the feet of others.

Spirituality involves others, not just ourselves: we let God love us in prayer, Eucharist, and spiritual practice, and then go out and share that love with a world hungry for God.

This book presents practical ways of spirituality drawn from the Scriptures and our tradition that help us truly mold into the image of Christ himself. We will look at conversational prayer, *lectio divina* (letting the Scriptures break open our hearts), contemplative prayer, imaginative prayer, and journaling—all spiritual disciplines, all practical and easy to learn.

A Guided Meditation

John 13:1-17

Sit in a comfortable chair. You may sit in silence or, perhaps, play a recording of Gregorian chant or soothing instrumental music. Let the stillness of God's love carry you into a deep place of calm.

In your imagination you hear the sound of bare feet on the floor. You look up and there is Jesus. He is carrying a basin of water. You look at his face and see the contentedness of a deep peace. His love becomes palpable. Your worries, sins, fears come to awareness in the presence of such love.

You know what you are supposed to do, take off your shoes and socks. He soaks the towel he holds with water from the basin and washes off your feet and ankles. You feel the warm and wet towel wash in between your toes. As he washes your feet, it is as though your heart and mind are also being washed. Tension flows out of you, the dirtied parts of your soul become clean and pure. Negativity flows from your body and soul into your feet, into Jesus' hands as they touch your feet, flowing from his hands into his body, where they disappear into the living flame of love that is his heart.

He finishes and hands you a towel, and says to you, "Go out and wash the feet of others. As I have loved you, so love one another, so love the least of these my brothers."

Chapter II

Conversing With God as a Friend

Once I heard the story of a young priest, Father Walter, who visited an elderly man in the hospital. When he entered the room, Father Walter saw that a chair had been moved to the head of the bed. He looked at the chair, then looked at the elderly man, then said, "I see I am not your first visitor today."

The man responded, "Oh no. That's Jesus' chair."

"What do you mean, 'that's Jesus' chair'?" Father Walter politely asked.

The elderly man replied, "When I was a teenager, I found it difficult to pray to a God whom I could not see. So I took the dilemma to my pastor and he suggested whenever I prayed, I put out an empty chair and imagine Jesus seated in that chair and talk to him like I would a friend. I have been doing that in all the six decades since then."

Father Walter did not hear from the elderly man for three days, and then got a call from the man's daughter. "Dad has died," she told him. "But there was something unusual when we found him; his head was resting not on the pillow, but on the chair."

He fell asleep on the lap of his Savior: *Even though I walk through the darkest valley, I fear no evil; for you are with me; your rod and your staff—they comfort me* (Psalm 23:4).

When I was around four years old, growing up in Columbus, Georgia, and skinned my knee or stepped on a tack, I would run to my parents. My mother would wipe away my tears with her gentle feminine hands; my father would wipe away my tears gently with his calloused electrician's hands. Isn't it wonderful to know that the same hands that fashioned and created the universe can one day wipe away all our tears forever?

Conversational prayer, talking to God as a friend, had enriched the elderly man's life for six decades. Though we don't always need to put out a chair to talk with God, God is the world's greatest listener.

Few things soothe and bring peace to our hearts more than a heartfelt talk with a close friend. We feel understood, accepted, listened to. Our isolation has been broken and we can connect to the world on a deeper level.

So it is with God. He already knows our needs, but he wants us to have the comforting experience of his listening to us.

Andrew, a middle-aged deacon I met while leading a retreat in the Midwest, approached me and asked to talk privately. His face showed the strain of someone who had just experienced a loss. I wondered if he was grieving the passing of a close relative.

He poured his heart out to me: the pastor, Father Bill, who had led his parish for 10 years, had been transferred to the other side of the diocese.

Andrew told me, "Father Bill had been especially close to me, my wife, and family. He was more than our pastor, he was our confidant. He had supper with us once a week and often came over after the last Mass on Sunday to watch football with me."

Father Bill had entrusted Andrew with many ministries. He had Andrew preaching twice a month, had him leading the parish's outreach to the poor, and appointed him co-leader of the parish's R.C.I.A. process.

Though this kept Andrew busy, he relished his work as a deacon.

The newly assigned priest, who wanted to be more involved with the parish, had cut Andrew's involvement. He changed Andrew's schedule, so that he preached only once a month. The new pastor wanted to lead the R.C.I.A. himself and hired a full-time director for the church's outreach to the poor. Moreover, the new pastor, more reserved than the previous pastor, did not make Deacon Andrew a confidant.

This all left Andrew with an identity crisis. He had overly identified his core being with the "things" he did for the parish. Moreover,

Andrew felt lost, not having a pastor as a confidant.

His stress over all of this was palpable. After pouring out his heart to me, he let out an audible sigh of relief. "It is so good to get all of this off of my chest. Except for my wife, I haven't had anyone to confide in about all these things."

I asked him about his prayer life, and he was honest with me. He had been so busy with ministry that he had stopped saying the *Liturgy of the Hours*, and now did little more for his devotions than say a decade of the rosary each day.

I explained to him that God is the world's greatest confidant, and went over with him some of the basics of conversational prayer. I also explained that, ultimately, prayer is not something we do, but something we become. God wants our whole lives to be a prayer.

I also mentioned that being a deacon is more than what we do, it's what we are. I pointed out to him that being a father does not consist of what we do, but what we are, so it is with being a deacon: "Taking on a heavy load of ministries does not make you a deacon; you are a deacon because of the sacrament of Holy Orders. The ordained deacon is a sacramental sign of the service of Christ, more than what you do."

Ordination "imprints a character," it doesn't just give you a function. As the *Directory for the Ministry and Life of Permanent Deacons* states, "Progress in the spiritual life is achieved primarily by faithful and tireless exercise of the ministry in integrity of life." As deacons, we are called to live our calling authentically, every hour of every day. There is no time off from being a deacon; and being a deacon does not cease when we cease doing work of ministry. We are deacons during our time at secular employment, during times with spouse and family, and during our times of recreation.

To live that "character" of deacon, it is important to have sacred time alone with God, to be in his presence. This is the time to talk with him as friend.

All believers, not just deacons and priests, need to take time each day to talk to God. No matter how advanced our prayer lives may be, we still need to engage God in conversation.

Conversational prayer is an intimate communication between friends. Jesus listens to us; we listen to him. We know that few things comfort us more than someone who lovingly listens. Jesus—the greatest listener, the greatest friend—experienced our fears, stresses, and worries. He understands us more than anyone.

Conversational prayer is not a new form of prayer. Its roots are ancient. The saints prayed that way.

Saint Alphonsus de Liguori, who could be called the patron saint of conversational prayer, lived in Italy during the 18th century. In his book, *Prayer as Conversing with God as a Friend*, published in 1752, he wrote: "God's heart has no greater concern than to love us and to make itself loved by us." This is the core principle of conversational prayer. He continues, "Always act toward God like faithful friends who consult with each other on everything . . . Accustom yourself to speak to God, one-to-one, in a familiar manner as to the dearest friend you have and who loves you best of all."

Not only do we speak with God in conversational prayer, God speaks to us. Saint Alphonsus writes: "God will not make himself heard by you in a voice that reaches your ears but rather in a voice that only your heart knows well."

How to Start a Conversation With God

Any prayer in which you converse personally with God can be called "conversational prayer." Rosalind Rinker, a former Protestant missionary to China, has written a score of books on conversational prayer, and has led hundreds of workshops on the subject. She worked closely with the Catholic bishop of Little Rock in teaching conversational prayer throughout the diocese and this work influenced the widely used Catholic "Little Rock Bible Study."

Like Saint Alphonsus, Rinker defines conversational prayer as a form of "spontaneous, childlike prayer, put out from hearts directly to the heart of Jesus." As much as possible, she urges people to pray out loud as they converse with God. I have found speaking the words just under my breath, moving tongue and lips a little, physically reinforces the prayer and works just as well. (Some people write out their conversational prayers.) The following steps of prayer were drawn from Rosalind Rinkers's four steps in conversational prayer.

1. *Jesus, you are here.* Recognize the Risen Lord's nearness. Welcome him out loud or silently in your own words. I often pray: "You are so near me, Lord, closer to me than my breath. Please open your listening heart to my prayers."

2. *Thank You, Lord.* Think over all the ways Jesus has loved and cared for you. Name some of those times, and thank him for them. Offer praise, worship, and adoration.

3. *Help me, Lord.* We take our needs to Jesus one by one. Tell him about your cares, admit your sins, and ask him for guidance.

4. *I pray for my brothers and sisters.* We move beyond ourselves to pray for others, thinking of their needs and cares. Pray for this hurting world of ours. Many deacons choose to do their conversational prayer at the time for

intercessions in Morning and Evening Prayer, tying their personal prayer to the prayer of the Church.

A Guided Meditation

Imagine Jesus is seated in a chair facing you. You see the light of heaven that surrounds him. Let the deep stillness of his presence enter your heart.

First, thank him for all the ways his love has helped you. Next, tell him your needs. Tell him about the ways you need his help in your life. Now, tell him about other people and situations that need his help. Pray for peace and justice. Pray that human life be respected and protected from the moment of conception until the moment of natural death. See the whole world surrounded and embraced by the light of Christ, which streams from his body.

Gently return to this time and rest in the stillness.

CHAPTER III

Lectio Divina: Letting Scripture Embrace Our Hearts

The men in my deacon class seemed joyful, eager and at peace, at the final canonical retreat just before our ordination. I had anticipated the same atmosphere 10 years later at a pre-ordination canonical retreat I was leading in the Northeast. The 12 deacon candidates seemed happy to be there, but, at times they looked weighed down, even anxious. At the first break, I found out why.

Two weeks before the retreat, Bill, a middle-aged dentist, found out his wife of 15 years,

Eileen, had cancer. It was uncertain at that time if her illness would be terminal or not, but the doctor said it most likely was.

Bill had come to the retreat only after several talks with his wife and much prayer. This was the first gathering of the class since the diagnosis, and his fellow deacon candidates expressed their rich and warm compassion to their confrere when they found out.

After supper the second night of the four-day retreat, Bill said to me, "Deacon Eddie, I see you will be giving a talk on *lectio divina* tomorrow. I have used *lectio* in my own devotions for three years now, since learning it at a seminar at my parish and God has especially touched me through that sacred practice, here on the retreat."

Bill went on to relate that he and his wife had shared many tears together in the two weeks since her diagnosis. By the time the retreat began, at least for a moment, they had come to a place of calm with one another. They had held each other in a long, silent, contemplative embrace just before he walked out the door. Both he and his wife shared a deep prayer life and, despite their agony, felt a sense of God's comfort.

But all that had unraveled once he arrived at the retreat house. Away from her presence, fear began to overwhelm him. So many thoughts and feelings ran through his mind. He wondered if he should be ordained or not. He knew if his wife passed away, he wouldn't be able to marry again and would be required to embrace celibacy for the rest of his life. He thought about raising their two teenage daughters alone, ministering to his parish without the support of his wife. He had decisions to make.

He told me that, during a long afternoon break that day, he went to the chapel alone with his Bible. He needed to feel God's touch, to hear his voice. In his agony, he turned to *lectio divina*, choosing Psalm 23 as his text.

Before he began reading, he settled in a front pew and turned his eyes to the tabernacle, settling down as much as was possible, considering his stress level.

He then read the psalm the first time, and all he felt were the knots in his stomach. Then, he read more slowly the second time, pausing between phrases. When he came to the phrase "I shall not want," the words rang true for him; they shimmered. He slowly, delicately whispered that phrase for a minute or two. Those simple words settled him, helping relieve the stress in his soul. Then subtly, organically, he changed the phrase to a prayer, "Lord, because of you, I shall not want," which he prayed over and over again, from the depths of his heart.

He continued reading the psalm. The words "green pastures" struck him, coming with a sense of God's grace. He then turned the phrase into a prayer: "You, and you alone, Lord, lead me to rest in green pastures." He paused in the silence, and then prayed from his anguish, "Lord, I don't want to be alone in that pasture. Can Emily be in that rest with me? I so dread the unknown that lies before us." As he expressed his pain, his load seemed to lighten a bit. He then pondered the meaning of "green pastures." He came to understand that, "this means a place of rest and regeneration, a place of God's goodness and grace."

He let his imagination enter into his rumination. He pictured himself resting in a bright green pasture on a sunny spring day. Then, he pictured Jesus coming to him, walking up to him and putting his hand on his shoulder. He later told me that he experienced a sense of deep tranquility and security. Bill settled into the depths of God's love, peace streaming through him. He rested in deep stillness for 15 minutes or so, feeling his connection with God grow stronger.

At the sharing time before the close of the retreat, Bill told all of us about his experience during *lectio divina* and the sense of God's nearness he had felt at the final Mass. He told the group that stormy and uncertain times lay ahead but, he knew that in the dark valley he and his wife were passing through, the Good Shepherd would be with them.

He said his time with God on that retreat had deepened his commitment to ordination. He put it this way, "Just as in baptism I was called to be a Christian, just as in marriage I fulfilled my call to be husband and father, I feel called to Sacred Orders. Whatever happens in my life, ordination is my calling. Even if I have to live that calling without a spouse, I live it with God and all brothers and sisters that form the Church."

What Is *Lectio Divina*?

Lectio divina is a Latin term that means "divine reading." *Lectio divina* is, in part, based upon the ancient Jewish practice called *haggadah*. Jews practicing *haggadah* would first memorize a passage from Scripture and then repeat it over and over again, slowly and softly, until the words made a home in the heart, transforming, refreshing the whole person. The Psalmist would seem to be describing this process in Psalm 118: "How sweet are your words to my taste, sweeter than honey to my mouth! Your word is a lamp to my feet and a light to my path" (vv. 103-105).

We find this practice first mentioned in the writings of the Church Fathers and Mothers of the third century, in the early years of monastic life in the desert. Saint Benedict of Nursia revised it in his famous *Rule*: "Listen readily to 'holy reading,' and devote yourself often to prayer." In the 12th century, a Cathusian monk named Guigo composed a book, *The Ladder of Monks*, suggesting *lectio divina* consisted of four steps, *lectio* (reading), *oratio* (prayer), *meditatio* (meditation), and *contemplatio* (contemplation).

The Steps of *Lectio Divina*

If we are to draw close to the heart of God, we must be willing to listen for his still, small voice (cf. 1 Kings 19:9-18). "They are the faint, murmuring sounds . . . [of] God's word for us, God's voice touching our hearts," observes Luke Dysinger, O.S.B., who describes *lectio divina* as "accepting the embrace of God."

Often, we want to read the Scriptures to obtain knowledge and meaning. We can never do without Bible study—the Bible is Divine Revelation, after all. For Bible study, we need to read Scripture in context and often consult good commentaries. *Lectio divina* is a different way of reading; a more intimate reading of Scripture, a reading with the heart. *Lectio divina* is also a way of prayerfully listening for the soft, quiet voice of God. Saint Benedict called *lectio divina* listening "with the ear of our heart." So, how does one begin? There are four simple steps.

Before you begin, take time to relax into grace. Settle into the silence. Take time to grow quiet in prayer, perhaps using the *Jesus Prayer* or by saying the *Hail Mary*. Take deep breaths and allow your heart to settle into a deep calm.

1. *Tolle, lege: Take up and read.* Select a passage of Scripture to read slowly. You may want to read it several times, each time a little more slowly and with longer pauses between lines and phrases, enabling the meaning to sink deep into the soul. Usually, most people read each passage at least twice.

Consciously slow your reading. The speed with which we read newspapers or articles on the Internet is not appropriate for *lectio divina*. One of the best ways to slow yourself down is to quietly read the passage aloud. Some people feel uncomfortable reading aloud, but give it a try. If you still feel uncomfortable reading aloud, just repeat the words slightly under your breath, move your tongue, but enunciate the words just under your breath. Read it slowly. Savor it. Let the feelings of the Scripture get inside you.

2. Next comes *meditatio*—ponder, ruminate, and meditate. Meditation pulls the latch of the truth, and looks into every closet and every cupboard. It labors to affect the heart. When a phrase resonates within us as we are reading, we "ruminate" on it, just like an animal chews its cud. We ponder it with the heart. As the famous 19th-century Baptist minister Alexander MacLaren put it, "The commonplaces of religion are the most important. Everybody needs air, light, bread, and water. Meditate, then, upon the things most surely believed, and ever meditate until the dry stick of the commonplace truth puts forth buds and blossoms like Aaron's rod. . . This great truth will shine into our gloom like a star into a dungeon."

3. The next step is *oratio*—prayer. Take time to converse with God on the themes of

the reading. Talk to him friend to friend. Enter into heartfelt talk with God as described in the previous chapter.

4. Deepen your contemplation (*contemplatio*). When you come to such a word or phrase that touches you, repeat it several times slowly. After you have savored and repeated the word or phrase, rest in stillness as long as it seems right to you.

This resting is a wordless basking in the presence of the One who loves us without measure. Your heart will instinctively apply the word or phrase to your life. When you come to a phrase or word that touches you, repeat it over and over again very slowly; it will take on a kind of anointing. For instance, if you are reading Psalm 23, "The Lord is my Shepherd, I shall not want . . . he restores my soul," the phrase "restores my soul" may seem particularly significant, something to savor. Just repeat that over and over, as long as the grace of the moment lasts.

When you are ready, close your Bible and close your eyes. A phrase or a word may so inspire you that you offer a prayer to God, and then perhaps hear his wordless “still small voice.” Don’t worry about having the “right” words to offer God. It is in the silence that we allow God to do what he wants, which is to simply love us.

This is a wordless prayer, a resting, a stillness. Such prayer is a gift of God and an invitation to intimate union. Anyone who has been in love knows that there are moments of wordless communion when hearts seem as one.

This may seem complicated, but it really isn’t. The parts of *lectio divina* don’t necessarily come in exact set stages. For instance, you might feel an inspiration to offer a prayer early in the reading; if you do, stop and pray. You may feel yourself drawn to repeat a word or phrase and ruminate over it. You may be drawn into the loving stillness of contemplation at any moment. If you do, stop and rest silently in God’s presence. You will know when it is time to begin reading the passage again.

A *Prayer*

Dear Lord, at times, my heart is troubled and afraid. There are times I stumble and can't find my way. Take my hand, then, and calmly lead me. May your words still me. May your Scriptures embrace me, reassure me, and bring me calm. For your Word is a lamp to my feet, a tender embrace for my heart, a pathway for body and soul. Amen.

Chapter IV

Letting the *Liturgy of the Hours* Form Our Hearts

I had hoped against hope the news would not come—the news that my dearly beloved first cousin, Betty, had died. She was 20 years older than me and, after the death of my own mother several years before (and since I was an only child), she had become the mother-figure in my life and the relative to whom I felt the strongest emotional ties. Everyone called her "Maw." We were close. She prayed fervently for the parish missions I led throughout the country. I had dedicated my most recent book to her. We spent all the holidays together with the rest of the family and when I was home, I saw her often. A giant-hearted, loving, and faith-filled Baptist Christian, she had changed the lives of everyone who knew her.

In the final stage of multiple myeloma, the whole family stayed with her. She lay on a hospital bed in the large living room of her house, suffering mightily, and often there were as many as 20 or 30 people with her. I spent hours a day there myself. An atmosphere of profound love filled her house in those last few days. I had the chance to tell her all the ways she had impacted my life.

In that tumultuous time, even though my head spun and my emotions rambled, the breviary was an anchor for me. I could not find my own words to pray because I was so distracted and, even though my emotions were drier than the desert when I prayed it, the breviary helped hold me steady during that time. She went into a coma and was not expected to live through that evening. But, she proved to be surprisingly strong and lived on, in a coma, for many days afterward.

She was still in a coma when the time came for me to fly to a parish mission I was leading near Killeen, Texas. I didn't want to go, but her daughter, Jane, and her two sons, David and Kirby, urged me to go: "Your prayers for her are just as good from Texas as they are in this living room," Jane told me. The people in Texas had waited a year for their parish mission and it would not be right to deny them.

I felt numb in Texas. I no longer had the warm support of my family in Georgia and the prospect of my cousin's passing was surreal. In denial, I thought that, if the phone didn't ring, maybe it meant she was going to wondrously survive.

Then my phone rang. My cousin Jane simply said, "Maw has died."

I didn't break down and cry with good grief; the news just anesthetized my soul further. I was breathing in a fog of unreality. I found it difficult to sink into the stillness of God, to talk to God, to sense him near. The words of prayer just wouldn't come.

So, I brought out the best help I had in that situation—*my breviary*. When everything was spinning around me, the breviary proved to be an anchor in my life.

After her death, when I could not grieve because I was too frightened to grieve, the words from the Responsory in *Night Prayer* for Friday comforted me: "Into your hands Lord, I commend my spirit." These became the words I needed to surrender to the reality of her death. Oh, how I wanted to be at that funeral, to be around others that had loved Maw and to connect with God. But that funeral was a thousand miles away, so the *Liturgy of the Hours* became the handclasp from God that shepherded me through that time.

The words from Psalm 88 flowed from my lips as I recited the *Office*: "Lord my God, I call for help by day; I cry at night before you. . . O turn your ear to my cry. . . My life is on the brink of the grave. . . I have reached the end of my strength. . . As for me Lord I call to you for help. . . Why do you hide your face?"

That psalm from *Night Prayer* gave me the words to say what it was like to lose Maw.

Those words opened up a channel inside for the grief to begin to flow. I began to cry some, then I broke down, which is what I had needed to do all along. The prayer from Jeremiah 14:9, "Do not forsake us, O Lord, our God!" rumbled around in my heart.

As I prayed the *Liturgy of the Hours* every day, peace began, a little at a time, to sprout in my heart. The everlasting arms lifted my heart.

I still grieve for her, even now, and I guess I always will. But in the midst of the grieving, the breviary also opened up for me channels for peace and joy. After a few weeks, I began to feel the presence and wonder again. The psalms and canticles of praise became a conduit of the sweet mysteries of God for my soul.

The prayers of the breviary have often steadied me in times of stress, gladdened me in times of sadness, called me to pray, and helped develop in me compassion for this hurting world. The praise from the psalms has carried me beyond myself into the wonder of the never-ending love.

"We pray the psalms to find a language for the encounter with God," Pope Benedict XVI said in a general audience. The prayers of the psalms speak directly to the human condition: sorrow, anguish, the need for humility and repentance, and the need to praise an infinitely loving God.

You may ask, "Why can't we just pray with our own words, instead of the *Liturgy of the Hours*?" One reason is that we would soon be repeating ourselves. Plus, when we feel the waves of dejection (or exaltation, for that matter), we often find ourselves at a loss for words.

John Brook, a convert from New Zealand, tells us:

> Without the *Office* our prayers can follow the same old track, saying the same things over and over again, boxed into our own small world. The *Office* explodes that box and opens us to experience the whole Church praying the mind of Christ, praying for the whole world for which he suffered and died.

Perhaps you feel out of step, as I do, when praying psalms of anguish, when everything seems bright and hopeful; or, for that matter, when we pray psalms and prayers of exultant praise during those times when our hearts struggle with sorrow.

Perhaps, the best perspective to have is that the rhythm of the prayers prepares our hearts for the other times when we do anguish or exult. C.S. Lewis aptly speaks to this, particularly to those times when our prayer lives are dry, when he wrote:

> When we carry out our "religious duties" we are like people digging channels in a waterless land, in order that when at last the water comes it may find them ready. . . There are happy moments even now, when a trickle creeps along the dry beds and happy the souls to whom this happens often.

The *Liturgy of the Hours* can help us with repentance, metanoia, the transformation of our hearts. For instance, "From my sins turn away your face. . . A pure heart create for me, O God, Put a steadfast spirit within me . . . My sacrifice, a contrite spirit, a humbled contrite heart you will not spurn" (from Psalm 51).

The words of the *Liturgy of the Hours* help us encounter the Scriptures as we pray. The *Liturgy of the Hours* primarily consists of Scripture. As we pray Scripture, those sacred words fill our hearts, like honey fills a comb.

Also, when you have extra time, use the insights of *lectio divina* as you pray the *Hours.* Read slowly, savoring each word. When a phrase or a word shines out, pray it softly, over and over again, to savor its holy nutrition. Be open to the silences and let the quiet carry you into the heart of God. Pause in silence often.

You may find you tire of so much praise in the *Office.* You may wonder if God has some insecurity, if he needs so much affirmation. As Daria Sockey in her wonderful book, *The Everyday Catholic's Guide to the Liturgy of the Hours*, suggests, it might feel as though, "The Lord, was eternally fishing for compliments, like a once-beautiful woman now past her prime."

We praise God not because he needs it, but because we need the wonder, beauty, and peace of being caught up in eternal love.

Perhaps the most important reason we pray the *Hours* is because Jesus prayed psalms and other texts from Scripture. Jews of Jesus' time often prayed memorized psalms throughout the day. And the Gospels tell us that he prayed Psalm 22 from the cross: "My God, my God, why have you forsaken me?"

As Pope John Paul II put it, when we pray the *Hours*, we pray "with the same words used by Jesus, present for millennia in the prayer of Israel and the Church."

The *Liturgy of the Hours*, as we use it daily, becomes a school of compassion in which we are taught to go outside ourselves to pray for others and this world of ours.

Chapter V

Opening Up to Compassion: The Challenge of *Diakonia*

It seems a lifetime ago, now. Still, some memories from my college days at Belhaven College in Jackson, Mississippi, where I was studying to become a Presbyterian minister, remain as vivid as if they happened yesterday, particularly a frightening dream I had of Christ.

In the 1960s, Belhaven was an all-white Presbyterian college. I loved Belhaven, and it was an excellent liberal arts school, where a high percentage of students prepared for ministry. The Scripture faculty modeled not only good scholarship, but holiness as well. They loved us, and poured their hearts into our formation. Amid the turmoil of the Sixties, Belhaven became a peaceful oasis for me.

For Mississippi, and much of the South, this was an era of violence against African-Americans and their allies. People were right when they described the state as "Mississippi burning." The Ku Klux Klan and those opposed to the goals of the civil rights movement murdered Medgar Evers and many more civil rights workers. The Klan and its allies burned 40 African-American churches and had infiltrated the local and state police. They bombed the Jackson synagogue, trying to kill Rabbi Nussbaum because of the hard work he and his congregation were doing to bring about racial justice.

For my first year or so at Belhaven, I put all this out of my mind and enjoyed the oasis of calm my school offered me. Then, I had a dream that turned my life around.

Prior to the night of the dream, I had ridden the bus from my parents' home in

Columbus, Georgia, to Jackson, returning to school after Thanksgiving break. Technically, the buses were integrated now. African-Americans, however, still sat in the back of the bus, if they valued their safety. There was a middle-aged African-American woman on the bus who was sobbing with nearly uncontrollable grief. Perhaps she had lost a loved one. At a stop, the white driver stepped back onto the bus and vigorously shook her, saying condescendingly, "Dry up, you are causing a scene."

I asked myself if I should go over and comfort her? After all, I was a candidate for the ministry, and comforting the sorrowing is what ministers do.

Then, fear struck my heart. What would the other passengers think of my going to the African-American at the back of the bus? Would they think of me as a freedom rider and beat me into a pulp? Would the bus driver stop and kick me off the bus? As much as I longed to go back to the woman and comfort her, I put my own safety above helping a fellow human being.

Two days after returning to Belhaven, I had a vivid dream of riding that bus again, only this time, it was Jesus seated in the back of the bus sobbing. A loud thunderclap from an autumn thunderstorm jarred me awake as I heard the words, "Find me at the back of the bus, or you won't find me at all."

The dream jolted me into realizing something essential was missing from my spirituality: identifying and showing "solidarity" with the "least of these."

That dream led me to fervent prayer, and out of that prayer, I saw I had to give and spend myself if I was to be a true servant. I involved myself in the civil rights movement in Jackson, meeting weekly with civil rights-oriented students from the different campuses in Jackson. At one point, I took part in an anti-Klan march. In those days, to be actively involved in civil rights in Mississippi meant you risked your life.

So many risked much more than I did, accomplishing much more. But at least I had begun on a small scale to realize what charity and service meant.

Belhaven finally accepted African-American students my senior year. Since then, the school has been a great example of racial harmony and equality.

Spirituality Is More Than an Experience of Personal Fulfillment

Often when someone first experiences God's love, he or she tends to view the spiritual life as a roadway to personal fulfillment and a happier family life. While prayer does lead to personal fulfillment, true prayer eventually draws us beyond the purely personal. We begin to see that our individual healing is tied in with the healing of the whole world. Only as I open up myself to the cry of the poor, to their pain, can the healing process begin within me.

Saint Paulinas of Nola captured our relationship with the poor in a timeless phrase: "[It is] association with the needy which heals our wounds." In short, the poor are our healing! They are our healing because their need for God, their need for grace, their need for love, is upfront. How easily we mask our own poverty. Each of us is poor. Each of us is broken. Each of us needs God's love and grace. Each of us needs other people. We try desperately to hide these needs from ourselves and from others. Our distractions and material possessions can easily become narcotics that keep us from feeling the pain and the needs that draw us close to God and one another. Perhaps that's why we fear the poor—because their need is so obvious.

The handicapped, the emotionally wounded, those denied justice, those who live in a state of emotional and physical starvation can't hide their need. If we dare make ourselves vulnerable to them, their need tears off our masks and we experience the depth of our own poverty. Vulnerability to the poor brings a wondrous grace to us. When our sister's pain and our brother's pain become *our* pain, we are drawn beyond ourselves.

Charity and compassion are at the heart of what it means to be a deacon. As part of our spirituality, we need to cultivate compassion when we pray.

Emptying ourselves for the sake of others in service is at the heart of what it means to be a deacon. Redemption involves the whole created universe. We are not saved alone; we are not healed alone. We are healed together in community with other human beings. We are saved and healed together with the whole universe. Saint Paul says, "He has made known to us the mystery of his will, according to his good pleasure that he set forth in Christ, as a plan for the fullness of time, to gather up all things in him" (Epheisans 1:9-10). And again, "He has put all things under his feet and has made him the head over all things for the church, which is his body, the fullness of him who fills all in all" (Eph. 1:22-23).

As deacons, we are called to let Jesus wash our feet, then go out and wash the feet of others. In his 1972 apostolic letter *Ad Pascendum*, Pope Paul VI called for the diaconate to be "a driving force for the Church's service or *diakonia* toward the local Christian communities, and as a sign or sacrament of the Lord Christ himself, who 'came not to be served but to serve.'"

Describing this service, the famed Scripture scholar Father Raymond Brown, S.S., wrote:

> In demeaning himself to wash his disciples' feet Jesus is acting out beforehand his humiliation and death. . .the foot washing is an action of service to others, symbolic of the service he will render in laying down his life for others; that is why Jesus can claim that the foot washing is necessary if the disciples are to share in his heritage and that it will render the disciples clean (from *The Gospel According to John*, 562).

I cannot be healed unless I am open to all creation being healed. That opening opens me to Christ's healing. But our society conspires to numb us. We place a high value on optimism, competition, and being on top of things. We hear so much bad news on television that we switch off our ability to feel much. And yet, the Apostle Paul calls us to weep with those who weep and rejoice with those who rejoice (Romans 12:15). Unless we are willing to feel the depths of pain, our ability to feel joy and laughter leaves us also. Part of our hesitation is that we see ourselves as vulnerable or fragile.

By taking in some of the pain of the world, we fear we would be shattered.

In his first trip outside the Vatican, Pope Francis visited Lampedusa Island, a part of Italy not too far from the African coast, where thousands of suffering refugees hope to begin a new life. Sadly, many are lost at sea on their way there. In his homily, Pope Francis spoke of the "globalization of indifference." He observed that the suffering of others no longer bothers us: "We are a society that has forgotten the experience of weeping, of 'suffering with'. . . The globalization of indifference has taken from us the ability to weep!"

During his visit to Lampedusa, Pope Francis offered a moving prayer: "We ask for forgiveness for the indifference toward so many brothers and sisters, we ask forgiveness for those who are pleased with themselves, who are closed in on their own well-being in a way that leads to the anesthesia of the heart."

An essential part of a true diaconal spirituality is letting God give us tender hearts that weep with and suffer with our hurting brothers and sisters. The meditation closing this chapter is intended for developing compassion for all who suffer, for our suffering world.

In *Despair and Personal Power in the Nuclear Age*, an excellent book on meditation for social activists, Joanna Macy says that, "The pain we feel for our world is living testimony to our interconnectedness with it. If we deny this pain, we become like blocked and atrophied neurons, deprived of life's flow and weakening the larger body in which we belong. If on the other hand, we let it move through us, we affirm our belonging; our collective awareness increases. We can open up to the pain of the world in confidence that it can neither shatter nor isolate us, we are not objects that can break. We are resilient patterns within a master plan." Ultimately, when we open ourselves to the pain of the world, we experience resilience—a resilience that comes from Christ's love that upholds and unifies all that is.

I hope that the following meditation can help you allow painful information to pass through you without it shattering you. A wise person once said, "Let all sorrows ripen in me."

Prayer can help us make rich compost out of the grief of the world. Meditative prayer can expand the breadth of our compassion. We accept the pain of the world and allow it to pass through us.

Prayer Experience*

Relax. Be still. Imagine that you are surrounded by the light of God's presence—an egg-shaped sphere of the light of his love surrounds you. Have a sense of that love encompassing you.

Now, allow images of your fellow human beings to emerge—images of people who are hurting, needy, alienated, sick, imprisoned, and on battlefields. There is no need to strain for these images. They are already there, waiting to come forward, by virtue of the fact that we are knitted with creation. Let them gather inside you like a dark liquid. Be open to the pain of all creation: the animals, trees, seas, and air.

Notice your breathing—your breathing in and your breathing out. Each time you inhale, you breathe in God's love; each time you exhale, you breathe out pain. Feel the pain leave you, absorbed by the light of God's love that surrounds. Breathe out your pain, the world's pain that you have taken on. Feel the light of God's love.

*This meditation is based, in part, on a meditation in *Despair and Personal Power in The Nuclear Age*, Joanna R. Macy (Philadelphia: New Society Press, 1983).

Deacon Eddie Ensley, Ph.D., is a permanent deacon in the diocese of Savannah and currently serves St. Anne Church in Columbus, Georgia. He speaks at retreats, missions, and conferences throughout the country. Deacon Ensley holds a master's degree in Pastoral Studies from Loyola University and a doctorate in Clinical Pastoral Counseling from Cornerstone University. He has authored more than 10 books on spirituality and pastoral care, and his most recent book is *Healing the Soul: Finding Peace and Consolation When Life Hurts.*

A noted retreat director, Deacon Ensley, along with Deacon Robert Herrmann, have also led deacon retreats and canonical retreats across the country. To request more information about their retreat offerings and Deacon Ensley's publications, please contact them at 706-322-8840, visit their website *www.parishmission.net*, or email Deacon Ensley at *pmissions@charter.net*.